Not College Material: From Janitor to Scholar

by: Terrance "Tuck" Tucker

ceived slight of an individual or organization is purely unintentional.

The resources in this book are provided for informational purposes only and should not be used to replace the specialized training and professional judgment of a health care or a mental health care professional.

Neither the author nor the publisher can be held responsible for the use of the information provided within this book. Please always consult a trained professional before making any decision regarding treatment of yourself or others.

Not College Material

Dedication

This book is dedicated to my parents and my son, my biggest influences. There are not enough words in the dictionary to explain what they mean to me. Everything I do is all for them.

Acknowledgements

I express my gratitude to God for the gift of life. Heartfelt thanks to my parents, the late Rev. James and Gussie Tucker, for instilling invaluable morals and principles in me. They always believed in me, even when faced with doubt. Their unwavering encouragement and prayers are missed, and I'm forever grateful for them.

Special appreciation to Craig Frierson, Quentin Merrill, Theodis Mullins, and Meesha Witherspoon for being pivotal in pushing me to write this memoir. Your constant support has been instrumental, and I am grateful for your confidence in me as an author.

A sincere shout-out to my brother, Author Zachary Middleton, for his mentorship throughout this entire journey. Your support and encouragement made this endeavor possible.

Thank you to my extended family and close friends, especially the Tucker and Salley family, for their love and unwavering support.

Finally, a heartfelt thank you to my son, Ajay Tucker, the primary inspiration behind this book. You are my everything, and I strive to make you as proud of me as my father made me proud of him. I love you.

In loving memory of my brother Jermaine Tucker—rest in peace.

Table of Contents

Not College Material

Chapter One:
The Chip on My Shoulder

I will never forget staring outside of my office window to get a better look at the impossible. Or at least what others said was impossible.

It happened towards the end of 2007. I remember the year because six months prior, I couldn't find a job in my chosen profession. I had recently graduated with my master's and performed well as a scholar. However, even after excelling in the classroom I discovered that getting a job in rehabilitation counseling wasn't easy.

I reached out to one of my mentors in professional counseling, Dr. David Staten. He helped me connect the dots while pushing me to network with industry leaders. As a result of that push, I received a call that resulted in the opportunity of a lifetime.

I received a call from a woman named Mary who had a sweet Southern accent. She asked,

"Is your name Mr. Tucker?"

"Yes ma'am," I replied.

"You need to come to DC so that you can talk to us," she said.

"I will be there tomorrow," I told her.

After that call, I gassed up my Cadillac, jumped on Interstate 95 and drove to Washington, DC.

When I arrived, I noticed that the office building was only two buildings away from the United States Capitol Building. When I walked into the building, and looked outside of the window, I realized that I was staring not only at the Capitol Building, but what others would consider unreachable or unthinkable. Prior to this moment, I was a janitor for five years. If offered this job, I was now about to be paid more than my parents combined salaries.

Oh… excuse me, I'm jumping into the story, and I have not introduced myself. My name is Terrance Tucker, and my friends call me "Tuck."

My friends would also tell you that I consider myself to be a bit of an underdog. I have been doubted and counted out many times in life. Many times, in fact the tattoo "chip on my shoulder," is tatted on my shoulder.

If I can be vulnerable for a second, then that underdog mentality is rooted in people telling me my entire life that I did not measure up. It started when I was a kid, struggling with a speech impediment. I guess I got the last laugh because now I am a motivational speaker and mentor program developer. I now get the opportunity to speak about life to young people in many cities all over. My speech, the thing people teased me about, is what I now use to empower people.

As I got older, people also teased me about not being smart enough. My guidance counselor told me that I was *"not college material."* I now have both my bachelor's and master's Degree from South Carolina State University. I believe it's the greatest Historically Black College or University (HBCU) in America. I also find it funny that schools and educational institutions now ask me to educate their students in life and leadership skills. It shows how life can surprise us, and how determination can change perceptions. It's a constant reminder that success isn't defined by others' opinions, but by our own determination and perseverance.

The worst way people counted me out was tied to personal behavior. When I was younger, I knew how to display good manners towards adults. However, as I got older, I hung out with the wrong crowd. I got in a lot of trouble trying to fit in, wanting to be accepted. Conversely, my life today is all about positive character and doing my part to instill that character into others. I get an opportunity to help people in my current vocation and through my passion as a leader of young men through mentoring.

I am writing this book because I want people like me to not be confined by society's limitations. I want to help people like me who've faced challenges and doubts, guiding them to recognize their true worth and potential. I want you to understand that you are valuable. That you have the potential to apply your academic and behavioral learning.

In this book, I am sharing my high and low moments. I want to share my milestones and my scars. I want to give you, the reader, my lived and learned experiences so that they can be better than me. If I can motivate one person, then I will have done my job.

My desire for you reading this memoir is that you will see how my life shifted when I started realizing how valuable I was. And how that understanding positively impacted me. It impacted my view of my education. It impacted my view of my peer relationships. Ultimately, it impacted the view of how I saw myself. I hope that, *Not College Material: From Janitor to Scholar*, will encourage the reader to recognize their own worth and in turn lead them to better value themselves.

This book is written for the person that struggles with self-confidence. This book is written for the person struggling with lack of support. This book is written for the person that may have a speech impediment. This book is written for the person that feels like they don't have a lot of options. This book is written for the person that does not believe that they are valuable. This book is written for a person like me.

For now, I need to start with the beginning. Let's go back to my hometown of Columbia, SC. Let's go back to the house of James and Gussie Tucker. Let's go back to my childhood.

Chapter 2:
Dad was My Clock, Mom was my Best Friend

To understand me, you must first understand that I am a family man. My family played a major role in shaping me into the man that I am today. I am a product of both the Salley and Tucker families. The Salley's are my mother's side of the family and the Tucker's comprise my father's side. I love my family; they were probably the only people that didn't count me out or dismiss me during tough times.

The first memories of my family begin with me growing up in Columbia, SC in the home of James and Gussie Tucker as the youngest of three. Many people don't grow up with having both parents in the home. I did and I am grateful for them both. I learned so much from them, character, hope, and service. When describing my relationship with my parents; my dad was my clock, and my mom was my best friend.

I use the word "clock" to define my dad because as a kid my sunrise and sunset were set by him. Every day he woke me up by shining his shoes. "Splik splock, splik splock, splik splock!" was the sound of the brush hitting the leather in the nearby room. The smell of black shoe polish would fill our home.

Even as a kid, I knew that the sound of my dad polishing his shoes meant that it was time for him to go to work. Since I knew that it was time for him to go to work, then that meant that it was also time for me to get up in the morning. His preparation for work signaled my preparation for school. My dad was the alarm clock that woke me up for each new day's adventure.

I also remember that his presence made me feel safe enough to go to sleep at night. I remember as a child my mom tried to get me to go to bed in the evenings. I couldn't go to sleep, even if I listened to her and laid in the bed motionless, I still couldn't doze off. I would lay in bed and wait for my dad to come home and set his keys on the kitchen table. The sound of my dad's keys would put me to sleep. It was as if the sound of his keys meant that the house was safe enough to sleep in, and that the house was now secure. My dad was my clock.

My father didn't talk a lot, but he spoke with his actions, he was a man of service. He was a bi-vocational pastor, and as a result, he was big into the affairs of the church. He always drove a Cadillac and listened to Gospel Music. He pastored Union Baptist Church in Calhoun County, SC.

When I was a kid, I knew that he worked for the post office. It wasn't until I got older, that I realized that he was one of the first black postmasters in our area. He fought against adversity and prejudice to achieve his position. However, he did his job with character and integrity. He took his position very seriously and I got to see his work ethic modeled through his everyday actions.

My father also showed me the importance of being a man around the house. He took care of paying the bills. He also took care of the cars in the home. He showed me how to change the tires. He showed me how to change the oil in the car. He was my first life skills instructor and model of manhood.

My dad was the definition of a man for me. In fact, one of my biggest measuring sticks in life is seen in his character and integrity. I have always wrestled with the fact that I thought that I could never be the type of man that he was. I will elaborate on this more later in the book.

I think that the character of our fathers has lasting implications in our lives. Perhaps it's because deep down a person knows that they will one day walk a mile in their parent's shoes. If blessed with the opportunity to grow up, then we will all have to forge our own paths. I had a great father that set the tone for my current success.

One of the greatest ways that my Pops modeled leadership was through his love of my mom. They were married for over 50 years. One of my most lasting memories was after he came home from work at the post office, he intentionally went to work on their relationship. He and she would often talk to each other once he got home. They had genuine affection for one another, and it showed.

When I recollect on my childhood experiences with my mom, my mom was my best friend. One of my fondest experiences was seeing my mom defend me when kids teased me about my stuttering. I have a stutter and I have stuttered since I was a child. The other kids teased me and sometimes the adults talked about me in a way that was not equal to the other students.

In first grade, the teachers wanted to put me in the "slow" classes, nowadays we use the more politically correct term remedial or resource classes. They were going to do this because of my stutter. As a result of my speech impediment, I felt uncomfortable talking in front of people outside of the family. Since I didn't talk a lot, my teacher thought I had mental problems and wanted me to place me in the alternative classes.

When my mom heard the news, she stormed down to the school and had a few choice words with the school's administration. I will never forget what she said, "There is nothing wrong with him! He doesn't want to talk to y'all! He talks to me all the time!" She demanded that the leadership take another look at me before making the switch. As a result of her prodding, they tested me instead of making a misinformed decision.

I passed the test with flying colors. I blew it out of the water! The only reason they mischaracterized me was because of my unwillingness to speak. They didn't realize that my refusal to speak was because I didn't want to be picked on because of my stutter. Sometimes we have a way of prejudging kids because we are not willing to interact with the complexity of their full stories. We are more focused on their "what's?" when really, we should ask questions about their "why's."

Throughout my young life, I infer most educators hated my mom for fighting on my behalf. However, my mom believed in me. Despite any obstacles, my mom believed that I was special, and she did whatever she could to improve my life.

In addition to my mother serving as my advocate, another influential support person that comprised my village was a teacher named Mrs. Garmany. Mrs. Garmany stood up for me during that time. When everyone else was dissing and dismissing me, Mrs. Garmany asked the administration to put me in her first-grade class. Everyone else saw me as a burden, she saw my speech impediment as both a challenge and an opportunity.

Mrs. Garmany cared about me. Even after passing her class in 1st grade, she still was very intentional about encouraging me throughout my elementary years. Many times, I remember her poking her head into my classes to see about my well-being from 1st thru 5th grade.

My relationship with Mrs. Garmany continues until this day, we are still friends. I am grateful for mentors like her. I am mentoring her grandson who is at the time of this writing, a college student at Alabama A & M. It's a full circle moment. All those years ago she took me under her wing and now I get to take her grandson under my wing.

Returning to the memory of my mother, like my father, my mom was also a woman of service. She worked as a secretary at Midlands Center Hospital for special needs patients for 35 years. She also worked as a part-time waitress for Seawells, which is a catering/banquet facility. In addition to these jobs, mom also worked in commercial cleaning where she cleaned churches and office spaces. Sometimes, I would help her clean just to spend time with her. We created a great bond during these moments. She was a hard-working woman, but she also was a woman that had a lot of love and compassion.

One fun memory that I have of my mother is her watching me play basketball. She would sometimes drive me to a nearby park to play basketball. She would stay in the car and read her newspaper and I would shoot basketball for the afternoon. She would go out of her way to make sure I had great childhood experiences.

Despite having a home with great parents, I still got into a lot of trouble. I grew up in a tough neighborhood. We were surrounded by nine Section 8 Housing projects. I would get in trouble for trying to defend myself. People would tease me and instead of making the decision to walk away, I would do everything in my power to defend my honor from their scrutiny. I would rather get spanked by my parents than have people say something about my character or intelligence that was untrue. As you can see, I have been fighting against what "they say…" for a long time.

I also got in trouble because I tried to hang out with the wrong crowd. Much of my trouble as a youth was linked to trying to be cool or trying to be perceived as cool. If I could get into a time machine and talk to the kid version of myself, (or to you the youthful reader), then I would say that you can be both cool and smart.

Your coolness should not be tied to being uneducated. Your coolness should also not be tied to trying to perform for peers who don't care about your personal growth. If you have a "friend" that is talking down to you because you are trying to better yourself, then that person is probably not your friend. Find friends that are trying to encourage you towards your positive goals, not ones that distract or promote negative behaviors and actions.

This was my childhood. All of which is foundational to framing the man that I have become. While I didn't grow up with a lot of money, I had something far more valuable, a great village. As time would show I would need that village to alleviate the burden of my soon coming teenage growing pains.

Chapter 3:
Teenage Growing Pains

One of my most important life lessons was learned one Sunday in my ninth-grade year while sitting in the security office of the Richland Fashion Mall. I decided not to go to church to hang out with my friends that morning. We had fun, played around, and enjoyed each other's company. Along the way, someone got the idea that we were going to steal clothes from the mall. Little did we know, we would be watched, followed, and caught by the authorities.

After we were caught stealing, the security officers called our parents. As I shared in the last chapter, my father was a pastor. Picking me up from the mall's security station meant that he and my mother would have to leave a church service in progress. That interaction would be one that I would never forget.

Before I share that story let me tell you about my teenage years. I am the youngest of three siblings. My brother loved music and my sister loved sports. She is the reason that I got into sports. Her passion became my passion. I soon discovered that I was good at sports. Sports was more than a hobby for teenage me, it became a form of identity.

Sports was a place that other students did not pick on me. I did not have to worry about stuttering when I was shooting a winning jump shot. Sports was also a place where I felt valued and not tolerated. Instead of avoiding me, other teens were asking me to be a part of their teams. As a result of my athletic ability, everyone wanted to be my friend.

Sports was also the first type of work that I loved doing. Each sprint, each workout, and each time lifting weights, held deep significance. As a teenager, I remember my work on the field of play mattered. It mattered because I felt like I was working in my area of talent. It mattered because I was contributing to a type of success that was bigger than my own. It mattered because it was a space in which I added value to other people's lives. It mattered because it was a fun or enjoyable way to spend my day and build new relationships.

One person that had a great impact on both my teenage years and my sports career was Coach Tim Gates. Coach Gates was an ex-Marine that was tough but fair. He had no problem giving his players constructive criticism. He could give you tough words, but you always knew that he cared about you.

My relationship with Coach Gates ended almost as quickly as it began. It almost ended because of the arrest that I alluded to at the beginning of this chapter, Coach Gates banned me from the gym that summer. I will never forget, when he got the news of my shoplifting he said, *"Out of all the guys I have coached, I think you could go the farthest. I just don't think you take life seriously."* Like I said, he gave us tough constructive criticism with care.

When Coach Gates banned me from the gym for an entire summer, it made me put my life into perspective. I was lost and miserable during this time, it made me reflect on my life and my choices. In addition to Coach Gates' punishment, I remember how low I felt from disappointing my parents. My mom was embarrassed and at that moment she said,

"I will be glad when (one day) I can look at you and you will make me proud."

I know for a fact that my mother loved me and was willing to stand up to anyone about her son. However, at that time I let her down, and when your mom tells you something like that you don't forget it. She even gave me the silent treatment for two weeks after it was over. That was hard to overcome, however my dad's punishment is what really did me in.

My dad worked many jobs, he worked with everything he had to provide for our family. His punishment was unique. As a result of my bad life choice that day, he decided to resign from one of his jobs so that he would be able to focus more of his time on me. Parents often say words like, "This punishment will hurt me more than it will hurt you."

In this case my dad punished himself and sacrificed to see better character in me. He was willing to sacrifice his career for me.

I remember thinking if he could sacrifice his job for me, then I know I can make the sacrifices needed to stay out of trouble. As I stated in the last chapter, my father's moral integrity was amazing. I often wondered how I would ever live up to his standard. If I can be vulnerable, then it's one of the reasons I have always struggled with pursuing personal accomplishments.

To this day I don't want it to be said that I am "better than" or more accomplished than him. My dad prioritized his son's well-being over a paycheck and that meant a lot to me. My father was a giant of a man and even as a teenager I knew that one day I would be tasked with following in his footsteps.

I also decided that because of that intervention, that I needed to change my friends. I remember the officers that arrested me told my parents, *"We can tell he is not a criminal, (or used to pursuing criminal behavior) because when we caught him, he never lost his manners."* Apparently, I treated them with reverence. I said, "Yes ma'am," "no ma'am," I respected them.

They communicated that they were used to interacting with disrespectful behavior when they apprehended shoplifters. In contrast, my posture of respect left a positive impression even when I was in trouble. I'm not saying that because I want a pat on the back, on the contrary, my shoplifting had serious implications. I could have landed in major trouble and/or severely damaged my reputation moving forward.

However, character matters and it is heavily influenced by the company you keep. I have a lot of love for the friends that I had at that time but even in high school I could see that they were headed in the wrong direction. As a result, I made the hard choice to find friends that were looking to make wise decisions.

My experiences in high school got better after that incident. I was a standout athlete, I played football, basketball, and track. I was voted the Most Valuable Player in football, and I made the All-State team in all three sports. For Senior superlatives, I was voted the best athlete in my High School and Most Popular. I had an enjoyable high school experience as it pertained to the "on the field" nature of athletics.

However, I had trials and tribulations off the field both in terms of behavior and academics. An example of this is the "McDonald's Story," it's a story that my former teammates and I laugh about to this day. However, when it took place, it was not funny. This happened later in my high school career. Some of my teammates and I decided to test Coach Gates. He had a team policy that we were not to leave campus between the end of school and the beginning of our basketball games. We broke that rule and decided to violate the team rules before a big game and drove to McDonalds.

Coach Gates found out that we violated the rules and gave us a pregame punishment for the ages. We had to run 50 football gassers. Gassers are when you run the horizontal length of the football field as wind sprints. We had to do 100 basketball suicide drills.

A basketball suicide is a line drill where you start at the baseline, run towards the shortest distance line, afterwards the runner returns to the baseline. You repeat this running structure until you touch all the floor length parallel lines throughout the entire length of the court. Once you have touched all the lines you have completed the first suicide. I infer that it's called "suicide" because the runner is inflicting the pain on themself with each stride and line touch.

When it came to that day's punishment, those examples were the tip of the iceberg. Coach Gates found other creative ways to make sure we understood the consequences of our actions. Even after receiving Coach Gates' punishment, I scored 17 points by halftime and my friend Maurice also scored

17 points. We sit back, joke, and laugh about it now but that day was no laughing matter, we learned an important lesson on the nature of discipline and consequences.

When it came to my work in the classroom, I will admit that I wasn't the best student. However, my poor performance was more rooted in my lack of effort and the fact that I didn't take my work seriously. I could have done the work better, but I didn't. The problem with any type of work or skill is that people tend to judge you by your performance and not your potential. I will never forget my guidance counselor who told me that I was "not college material." Those words were heavy for me because my parents did not go to college.

My guidance counselor was college educated and in a position of authority, so at the time I listened to her. However, the problem with her assessment was the fact that it was not a measurement of my true capacity. It's one of the reasons I believe mentorship is so important, mentorship helps cultivate young people to live up to their potential.

If you are a mentor reading this book, then remember that your words and actions matter. As mentors and youth workers, we have the power to speak life and encouragement into the young people in which we help. We can also limit them when we carelessly categorize them.

After graduating from high school and accepting the belief that I was not college material, I decided that I would join the military. However, my recruiter told me that to be eligible I would need to pass the ASVAB test. I took the test, but I did not do my best. I remember I went through the motions and decided to bubble in the answers. My recruiter was pissed when she got the scores back. She told me that I wouldn't be able to get into the military because I didn't score high enough on the test. It looked like I wouldn't become a military man after all.

Two weeks after that rejection, the date was September 11, 2001. On that day, two planes flew into the World Trade Center as an act of national terror. As a result, the United States was about to go to war. The recruiter that once told me that I had been rejected, immediately changed her tune. She was now doing everything in her power to get me to join the military despite my low-test scores. By that time, my mother would have none of it. It was one thing in her eyes for me to want to go into the military during peacetime, it was another thing for me to go into the military during a time of war.

Since I wouldn't be going to college or the military and I didn't have any professional skills, I had to focus on manual labor. I started out by working to load trucks. The work was difficult and despite being a lifelong athlete it put major pressure on my back. My doctor insisted that I stop working due to having numerous back spasms. The doctor got a lawyer to notarize a letter, which made my employer accept a notice.

The employer didn't want to accept the notice due to being short staffed, but the notarized letter displayed the severity of my issue. I think that this is a life lesson for anyone that is working a job that is destroying them personally. Having this specific job was not worth the long-term back problems caused by this role.

While most of my former employers would tell you that I always sought to demonstrate good character while on the job. I must admit that there was one work experience where I did not demonstrate positive character. It happened when I got a job at a major tire service company. The supervisor tried to embarrass me publicly.

Part of the reprimand was that the supervisor wanted me to wear my goggles and a back brace. During a heated moment, I acted out of character. I threw my goggles across the room when I told the supervisor I was quitting the job. Not something that I am proud of over a decade later, however, it did happen. I wish I could say that it was the end of the story.

After leaving the tire company, I submitted my application to a major department store. The hiring manager relayed the fact that they had some bad news. They said that my application was placed on a 10-year application ban. I didn't understand why this happened. I had never worked there before; I couldn't figure out how I had been banned. The leadership explained that the large department store was an affiliate business to the tire company in which I had my unruly exit.

When I was banned from the first store, I was banned from the second because they were part of the same system. The moral of the story is your reputation at work can follow you. Every situation won't be like this one, but employers have a way of talking to each other. When it comes to workplace professionalism, how you start is often as important, (if not more), than how you finish at a place of employment. Choose wisely.

All these work experiences were important in my career story. Sometimes you need bad experiences to show you what you don't want to do in the future. These experiences were also important because they led me to work a job that I would never forget, working as a janitor in a Columbia, SC based high school. I learned so many life lessons as a janitor. The biggest came in the form of a conversation that helped to form my outlook on life and leadership.

Chapter 4:
The Question I was asked When I Worked as a Janitor

I worked as a janitor for three or four years after graduating high school. I enjoyed the job. My mother also worked as a janitor in the evenings on a part-time basis. It is an important job that adds value to every student, teacher, and parent associated with that building. However, my issue was that I never realized that I could pursue other options.

I became the leader of the school's janitors, but I got paid a wage rate of $10 an hour every week, which was a little higher than minimum wage. I didn't mind the wage because I didn't have to pay any bills.

However, there was not much room for financial advancement in this position and eventually I would need to move out of my parents' house. Despite those obstacles, I would still be a janitor if it weren't for a conversation that I had with the leader of my school, Principal Dr. Witt.

I'll never forget that conversation, I was mopping the gym floor. Dr. Witt walked up to me and asked,

"What are you doing here?!"

"What do you mean? I asked, "It's my shift!"

"No, I mean what are you doing as my lead janitor?" Dr. Witt asked.

"It's my job!" I told him.

"You need to be in college somewhere," was his next response to me.

"Well, Dr. Witt, my guidance counselor told me that I am not college material." I replied.

"Let me explain why you are college material. You are on time every single day. You never leave until the job is done. When these teachers talk about you, they are always talking about your character. You are always saying 'yes sir, no sir' or 'yes ma'am or no ma'am.' You are a hard worker. That is what makes you college material."

What Dr. Witt was helping me see is that being college material is more than just having good grades. It's the mindset that leads a person to work hard for their grades. It's the mindset that leads them to be responsible. It's the personal character that allows them to prioritize their work. Being successful in college is about being present and putting in the necessary work needed to accomplish one's task.

The "present" he was talking about is not just showing up in attendance while going through the motions. He was speaking about being both in attendance and living life with a present sense of intentionality that encourages a person to live their life to their fullest potential. This was the first time a black man said this to me, and I still value that conversation to this day.

While that conversation was influential in making the hard decision to go back to school, going to college was difficult for me to wrap my mind around because neither my mom nor my dad went to college. This discussion heightened the lie that I was telling myself that I was not good enough. People in the academic community call this imposter syndrome.

This is a little different from other people telling me that I was not good enough. The difference was that I started believing that I was not good enough. Before, the voices of doubt were coming from others, now the voices of doubt came from me. I didn't believe that I could measure up to the standard of being a successful college student.

I am grateful for my aunt Dr. Judith Salley. My aunt is an incredible academic and community leader. She believed in me and was intentional about changing my perspective. She did everything in her power to convince me, including helping me with the application and mentor me through the college admissions process. She, along with Dr. Witt, did everything in their power to get me into college. Through their help, I was able to get into what I believe to be the best HBCU in America, SC State University. Go Bulldogs!

Soon after those interactions I was ready to start a new journey. I was ready to begin my college experience as a 22-year-old freshman.

Chapter 5:
What my grandmother taught me about Discipline

My first year in college was an adjustment period. It was a tough year, but it changed my life. I learned things about myself and my work style that I still implement as a professional today.

I arrived at SC State University's campus on academic probation, and I had to work hard to maintain my status as a student. I am grateful for my aunt because her assistance and guidance through the process was essential. She helped me understand the different world, that is adjusting to life on an HBCU's campus.

Initially, I could take no more than 12 hours at a time. I couldn't make any mistakes. In addition to my academic guardrails, I also had to volunteer my services in the cafeteria. I also had a financial provision that was connected to my ability to maintain my grade point average (GPA). I knew that if I was going to be successful at SC State, I would have to work hard in many ways.

All these changes interrupted my life. However, they were not the biggest adjustment that I had to make. The biggest change in my first year was that I had to live with my grandmother. My grandmother was my heart! I never knew my mother's mom because she died when I was only three years old. However, my father's mother was Vernell Tucker. She was born in Cope, South Carolina and lived there her entire life. Cope is located a few miles from Orangeburg, the location of my university's campus. When she heard that I was going to SC State she told me that, "I had to stay with her to focus."

My grandmother was a devoted Christian that loved her family. She showed me the power of prayer. I now pray for myself in contrast to expecting others to pray on my behalf because of her. She gave me an 8:00 p.m. curfew each night and each morning at 6:00 p.m., she made me feed the pigs and chickens she raised. She had no cable television and she lived so deep in the country that it was hard to get cell phone reception. Living with her was a priceless experience that I will never forget.

My first year in school I went to class, I went to work, and I went home. That was the bulk of my life during my freshman year at SC State. The negative of that lifestyle is that I did not have a vibrant social life. However, the positive was that that regimen taught me discipline.

I think even bigger than my grandmother's approach to discipline was God at work slowing me down. I think that sometimes God has a gracious way of slowing a person down. This is what I believe He was doing to me at this moment. I am now grateful for this period. I learned a lot.

Another important memory from this period is that I was willing to receive help from a peer or a person that was around my age. I was assigned a mentor by the school named Crystal Smith; she was a student from Trinidad. I had to go to her sessions Monday through Friday every day as a first semester student. She was tasked with helping me, a 22-year-old freshman, that read on an eighth-grade level. She was very patient with me.

Through her help and the help of a caring administration, I was able to adjust to campus life. I can't overstate their significance because it's important to note that my home life was not like many other students. Her tutoring helped to better give me the support system I needed to excel.

Freshman year was also important because I learned how to "lose weight" and find my "GPS." These are two metaphors that I use to describe how my relational patterns changed for me to be successful in college. When I describe losing weight, I am talking about losing bad habits that impeded academic progress. When I talk about my GPS, I am referring to associating with people that are heading in the right direction. One metaphor involves saying no and the other saying yes to a new way of living.

I had to lose the "weight" of bad habits that weighed me down while I was in high school. Some of those habits include associating with certain people, by this time many of those high school friends continued the pattern of making bad choices and were caught up in the street life. It was important that I had to make the sacrifice of letting those friends go. I also had to let go of the low expectations of personal character, ability and discipline that I had set for myself in high school. The old Tuck had to stay home.

When I talk about finding my GPS, I am not talking about the Global Positioning Systems that we often find in our cars and phones. I am talking about the leadership and direction given by high character friends. Because I started college at 22, my former high school classmates were going to be seniors that year. They were getting ready to end their college years as I was just beginning mine.

My GPS friends were Kodi Brown, Courtney Fulton (who was also another tutor), Delvon Harling, and Aukeaus Solomon. I am grateful to each one of them because they treated me well. They didn't turn their backs on me or try to avoid me. They helped me with my syllabus, they showed me how to read my schedule, and they helped me navigate the campus. They helped me discern which other people to hang out with on the campus. Their friends became my friends, and we were all one big family.

The two teachable moments that I learned from my GPS were 1. The friends that we choose matter greatly. 2. We have a tendency of becoming like the people that we hang out with or spend the most time around. I also think it's important to note that we had a lot of fun. While my friends were wiser, it doesn't mean we didn't have an enjoyable time. However, having wiser friends helped me see that college and success in life at any level is based on not only having balance, but also being serious.

I remember feeling that my first year at SC State was a testing period for me as a student. I compare it to being a rookie student athlete that starts playing sports. I wanted to know if I belonged or could cut it on this level. I am happy to report that I did well that first year. My first semester (GPA) was a 2.9 and as a result I no longer was on academic probation. The following semester I also did well in the classroom.

My tutor Crystal, who played a major role in building my confidence, cried when she got the news of my good grades. She cried because she knew how far I grew in a year. When I met her, I was reading on an eighth grade reading level and through the grace of God, focus, discipline and a lot of hard work, I was able to excel as a student. My whole life I had been praised for my athletics. My first year at SC State was truly a display of my ability to be "college material."

My last memory of my freshman year was a full circle moment that occurred in the campus bookstore. Years ago, when I attended college, many students still bought the physical copies of the textbooks in contrast to purchasing digital resources. At the end of the semester, we had the option of selling the textbooks back to the school at a fraction of the original purchase price. As I was selling my books back to the bookstore, I ran into an old friend. I encountered Coach Gates. He gave me a big hug upon understanding my academic progress and said with sincerity, *"I knew you could do it!"*

If there was one thing that I could pass to every student reading this book, then it is that same encouraging belief. I know that the people capable of reading this book can excel in school. Please don't read this book as a hero's tale. I am sharing my story with the posture of if I can do it, then so can you! In the same way that Coach Gates told me and believed in me, I also believe that you can do it too!

Chapter 6:
Manhood Lessons Learned as a Sophomore in College

If my freshman year was about my growth academically, then my sophomore year was about my growth as a man. By that year, I was committed to SC State because I had beat the odds, but I still had some growing to do.

One major example of my manhood growing pains is seen in my introduction to a man named Mr. Gene Breeland. As a SC State student, one enjoyable activity that helped build camaraderie amongst students on campus was intramural athletics. We had a great time battling in Dukes Gym, a historic gymnasium that is located near the center of campus.

Mr. Breeland was the staff member that supervised our activities within the gym. My friends, family, and peers would tell you that I am very professional and well-mannered in most settings. However, I have the tendency to talk a lot of trash when I play sports. Sometimes when I talk trash, I use street or profane language.

On one day I was using a lot of street language. Mr. Breeland overheard my language and called me into his office. He said, *"If I hear you cuss one more time, then you got to go!"* I heard what he said, then promised him that I wouldn't use foul language again then returned to the basketball court.

Soon after our conversation the game got heated again. Instead of keeping the promise that I made to Mr. Breeland, I went back to cussing. Even though I didn't keep my promise to Mr. Breeland, he kept his promise to me. Mr. Breland responded to my profanity by saying, *"Son, you got to go!"*

I did not respond to my punishment appropriately. Perhaps it was because others were watching, or maybe it was the way that I felt at that moment, but in either case I got super disrespectful with Mr. Breland. He was trying to help me, but now I didn't see it that way. I let him have it by continuing to be argumentative and disrespectful. True to his word, he made me leave the gym.

I felt embarrassed after the incident. My parents did not rear me that way. I went home and sat in the dark. I felt bad because I knew better but I did not live up to my capabilities.

Three days later, one of my professors, Dr. Fishburg explained that part of my academic requirement was to receive approved hours from the PE Department. I remember asking him, *"Who is the supervisor of this section within the PE Department?"* He responded, *"Mr. Gene Breeland."*

Cue the theme music! If I wanted to advance in my major, then I would have to face the person that I disrespected. It was just like the moment working with the tire company when I was a teenager. My past actions didn't die.

Our negative actions have a way of outliving the moment. The way that you treat people matters because it has the potential to form and shape your reputation. You can do many things right but the moment you act up, that can be the way you are perceived. Your reputation impacts relationships, your hiring potential, and other factors.

Soon after speaking with Dr. Fishburg, I went to find Mr. Breeland. Through much shame and embarrassment, I had to apologize for my actions. Mr. Breeland could have been salty and treated me horribly, but he didn't, he responded in an opposite fashion. He said that he knew another person who also happened to banish me from another gym many years prior. Coach Gates.

He said that Coach Gates told him who I was and how proud of me that he was. Once again, reputation helped form a future relationship. Instead of hanging the past incident over my head, Mr. Breeland not only signed off on my hours. He went on to give me a job.

Can you imagine that? The person that I had disrespected, was also the person that became one of my first mentors outside of my family. Mr. Breeland became my "Pops" around campus. He took on a big brother/mentor role. He trusted me to lock up the gym. He left me in charge many times and empowered me to be a leader on campus. My relationship with Mr. Breeland changed my time as a student and helped me to grow as a man.

Manhood is more than having the right grade or being successful in the achievements of life. Manhood has a lot to do with personal character. In this scenario, my past actions built my reputation through a prior relationship with Coach Gates and Mr. Breeland. My reputation walked into the room before I did. My personal character was put on display with my actions with Mr. Breeland. The first encounter had the potential to create a beef with a person that would become like a father figure.

As a man, I had to face my mistake and apologize. I saw manhood modeled in the way that Mr. Breeland showed me grace. He forgave my past offense and gave me a second chance. I am grateful for men like Mr. Breland that played a part in mentoring, molding, and shaping me into a better man.

Chapter 7:
Graduating to Tears

I will never forget my college graduation. When you graduate college, it is the culmination of all the hours you have worked, studied, and devoted expressed in one event.

Like a flashback in a movie, when I reflect on my graduation, I think back to my entire academic journey. Starting with being told in elementary school that I should have been learning disabled. I then flash to my guidance counselor telling me that I was not college material. Then I remember my momma telling me, *"I will be glad when I can look at you and feel proud."*

I then think about the many hard labor jobs that I worked before enrolling in college at 22 years old. Along the journey, I reminisce on the life lessons that I had learned with mentors and friends. All those moments made my family's cheers feel that much sweeter during my graduation.

However, the climax of the graduation experience happened when I interacted with my father. If you recall in the beginning, I stated that my father was my clock as a child. He set the tone for me and my family. Not only did he set the tone, but he was also a man of incredible character. He was willing to give up one of his jobs so that we could spend more quality time when I was growing up. His integrity is still and will always be my benchmark for manhood.

My father was a giant of a man. He was a giant in character, and he was also a larger man, he was 6'6 280 pounds. While I have seen my father do a lot of great things, the one thing I have never seen my father do is cry. Never in my life could I recall my dad crying prior to that moment. On the day of my college graduation, my father cried tears of joy. `At that moment, I had made him and my mom proud of me.

Graduation was more than a ceremony for me. It was a display that I had not accepted other people's narrative. Other people told me that I was not "college material." My graduation was a display that I didn't believe what they said about me and for the rest of my life I have the evidence of my diploma to prove it.

Many years after graduation, my father expressed some of his feelings surrounding my life at his church. The sermon focus was the Scripture, Matthew 19:26, "26 But Jesus looked at them and said, *"With man this is impossible, but with God all things are possible."* In this sermon, he used my life as an illustration of what God could do. My dad said, "They told me that my son wasn't going to be anything!" That shook my soul. It was proof that he had heard the naysayers also, but like me, he didn't believe them.

I also got to see how being rebellious and not living up to my potential, weighed on my parents. I may have made some mistakes in life, but those mistakes were not his fault. To me, he was the best dad ever. My dad gave me character and I am grateful for what he instilled in me.

Every day I still carry on the legacy of his character. I try to live as a man of honor and encourage others to do the same. Little did I know that I would need that character once again as a student. I thought my academic journey was complete after obtaining my bachelor's degree, however as I would soon see, I still had more to learn.

Chapter 8:
What is a Master's degree?

Soon after I graduated college, I was hanging out with two of my friends who had professional aspirations. For this book, I will refer to them as "Big 'Cuz' and "Little 'Cuz.' It was through my conversations with them that I first heard about the possibility of pursuing a master's degree.

I had no knowledge of what a master's degree was. They gave me an understanding that I would need to go back to school for two years. My initial reaction was "Oh, No! I don't want to spend more time in school!" I thought I was finished with the classroom.

However, I spoke to my aunt, Dr. Judith Salley and she was giddy about the prospect of me getting my Master's. My mother also thought it was a good idea and encouraged me to pursue it. She worked for the Department of Disabilities for 35 years and understood its value. I also learned that it was a helpful degree to have in my chosen profession.

My decision to pursue the Master's was solidified when I met with a man named Dr. David Staten. He took his time and explained what it meant to have a Masters. As a result of that conversation, I knew that he would need to be a friend and mentor in my vocational journey.

After I decided to get my Master's, I learned that I would need to pass the GRE exam. GRE stands for the Graduate Record Examination, it's a standardized test that many universities require students take prior to entering their master's programs. I studied the test in a Barnes & Noble with a friend named George White and my then girlfriend. I was nervous about the test, but faced my fear and took it. A short while later, I was notified that I made a high enough score to get into the master's program at SC State.

Once again, I was going to be a student. The work was difficult, and I had a tough time keeping up. That is when I met my second mentor in the profession Dr. Hollis Staten who happened to be the wife of Dr. David Staten.

Just like in the situation with Mr. Breeland a few years prior, I met this mentor through a bad situation. I was in her class, and I thought I was slick. I thought I would try to make a cheat sheet. She intercepted my plan and gave me the pep talk of a lifetime.

She pulled me aside outside of class time and called me out. When I denied it, she told me that, "either I man up or she would kick me out of the program." I confessed that I made a cheat sheet because I thought I needed it. She asked me "why?" I said, "I don't think that I have what it takes to keep up with the rest of the students. I don't want to fail." She then said these honest yet life affirming words, "You are more than enough, you have what it takes, but you can't cheat your way through."

Later in the conversation, she went on to say that I would need to dress the part. At that time, I was wearing my hoodies and sweats. She encouraged me to dress like the people in my profession and buy some collared shirts and slacks. She also gave me her office hours and told me to come see her for extra instruction, if I was struggling in the future.

I took her advice and put away the cheat sheets. I bought a bunch of professional attire and began to take the process seriously. I left that interaction with an understanding that part of being more than what is expected, is confidently walking towards my goals. That means hard work, professionalism, and a willingness to not believe the lies that I was still telling myself. I am grateful for her words. She, like her husband, Dr. Staten are still both my mentors today.

Several months after that moment of truth, I began seeing the fruits of my labor. In 2007, I was able to turn things around and I was named the Scholar of the Year. I came in struggling but graduated with my Masters having a 3.2 GPA. I also learned that the benefit of having a master's is not only scholastic. I would soon find out my master's also influenced my earning potential and credibility as a professional.

I went from not knowing what a master's degree was to getting accepted into a master's program. I went from thinking I had to cheat to excel to understanding that I was "enough." Not only was it enough, but I had the qualities needed to be a standout student in this field and I was excited about the prospect of the doors that this master's degree would open.

One transferable lesson from this experience is that it is wise to embrace learning opportunities that will stretch you to grow. Experts call this growth mindset, it's the willingness to continuously learn and grow no matter your age or past experiences. Growth mindset extends past the classroom; it is what fuels my desire for learning through relationships, exposure to new opportunities and through travel. Little did I know at the time, but my master's would open doors to all three of these growth areas.

Not College Material

Chapter 9:
The New Doors Opened Through Travel

One of the ways that I continue to grow as a leader is through travel. Travel is a way that leaders can experience the world, meet new people, and be exposed to new opportunities. One of the first places that I began to travel was in graduate school.

Before going to graduate school, I didn't leave the South. I went as far as North Carolina for family trips, but no further than that. Part of my graduate school scholarship was that I would be able to go to professional conferences. I got to go to San Diego, California, and Washington DC.

Washington, DC was quite a memorable experience. The conference was held during a time when a lot of events were going on in the city. After first communicating with my graduate school advisor, I decided to explore Washington, DC after the conference sessions were concluded. I got to attend Howard University's Homecoming, which is famous even amongst other Historical Black Colleges or Universities (HBCUs). I got to ride the DC Metro where I saw a diverse picture of DC culture.

DC is seen by some to be the "Mecca" or center of black people in America. What stood out to me about DC was that I saw many black leaders in the area. This experience set the bar high for what black professionals could become in America.

San Diego was also an amazing experience. I went from the East Coast to the West Coast. It was one of the first times I had ever been given a stipend for my travel. A stipend is when your supporting organization gives you a specific financial allowance for meals or detailed expenses when you travel. During that conference, I was able to build some long-standing relationships.

One of the reasons that I was able to build those relationships was due to the guidance of my mentors, the Staten's.

Dr. Hollis-Staten gave me a lot of wisdom. She would ask, *"What is different about you in contrast to anyone else? What about you would stand out among everyone else?"* She was trying to get me to understand what experts call my unique value proposition. What is it about me that adds value to my potential employer?

Dr. David Staten made sure to emphasize the importance of networking. Networking means to build relationships, exchange information, and cultivate professional contacts in a similar or related field. I think networking is paramount to anyone's success. Dr. Staten challenged me to return from the conference with no less than ten business cards. I had to initiate connections with complete strangers.

I have a confession, even though I am now a motivational speaker, and I must build new relationships all the time, I struggle with the anxiety of building those relationships. I was like a fish out of water. I was new to it all and I had to introduce myself to new people. However, I am grateful for the challenge. I had to face my fears and walk across the room to talk to someone new.

Along the way to building those relationships and getting the business cards, I learned that the trick to networking is being proactive. Don't wait for the perfect moment, start the conversation, introduce yourself, and connect the dots through shared interest.

It's also good to go into a networking event or a job interview knowing your value and believing in what you are selling or presenting. I also recommend having a resume or credentials that match your ambition. One thing is for sure, and two things are for certain, people will find talented professionals. There are opportunities out there, but you must take the initiative. Put in the work and network!

One great thing that came from the "ten business cards" challenge is that I was hired by one of the guys that gave me his business card. As I expressed in the beginning, getting hired was not easy but it all worked out in the end. A big part of finding a job, growing as a professional or exposure that comes through travel comes because of taking the first step.

The transferable lesson that comes from this chapter is I would encourage you to find a mentor. I have been blessed to find great mentors that have helped me in life and in career. Who are those people for you? Think long and hard about the people in your life that you trust, that are wise, and are willing to share their wisdom with you. Consider life mentors that can help you with your general daily existence.

Also consider finding career mentors like the Staten's have been for me. Who are some people that are a few years ahead of you as it pertains to career or vocational growth? Reach out to these people, ask for a meeting, and listen to any insight that they offer. Put the ball in their court as it pertains to whether they will mentor you long term.

However, be clear and share that you respect them and would appreciate it if they would consider mentoring you. Some people are busy and don't have the time for weekly or monthly mentoring. However, even in that one meeting or a willingness to respond via e-mail they may give you insights and wisdom that may take you years to master independently.

I would also echo the Staten's' advice to me. What is your unique value proposition? That means do some self-reflection and discover what are the parts of you that are unique and distinct to you. What aspects of you or your skills add value to others or a potential employer? When you are in a networking scenario, I encourage you to walk across the room and build relationships.

If setting the goal asking for and retrieving ten business cards helps you, then start there. If you struggle with getting started with the first conversation, try this, "Hi my name is (your name) how are you doing?" Actively listen to their response, and then respond. Where are you from and what do you do?

This may be the start of a great friendship or business relationship. Other great opening questions include, what is your story? How did you hear about this event? How are you connected to the host? What do you think about this weather we are having? What do you do for fun (or what do you do when you are not working)?

If I am getting too "teachy" in this chapter, forgive me. I have a passion for mentoring and helping to improve the lives of others. As a matter of fact, let me tell you about a mentoring organization

that I started and actively participate in named the
TUCK Project.

Chapter 10:
The ᴛᴜᴄᴋ Project

In addition to my work as a behavioral health therapist, I also launched a mentoring program named the TUCK Project. TUCK stands for "Together Uplifting Community Kids."

I don't like drawing attention to my service work; however, the organization is a structured way that I seek to be a mentor to others. As this book has shared how many people have mentored me and invested in my development, I seek to be a beacon of hope for the next generation.

The TUCK Project organization focuses on mentoring, empowerment speeches, and helping the homeless. The efforts are focused on downtown

Columbia, SC and downtown Augusta, GA. I also think it's important that these young men receive life skills training.

The reason I was compelled to start this organization is rooted in my own upbringing. I saw a lot of young men who didn't have mentors make bad decisions. I saw a lot of young men who were upset because their dad was not in their lives. I saw guys end up homeless, some guys were killed due to poor decisions. I saw a lot of wasted talent and I don't think it was their fault. I said many years ago if God gave me the ability to be in a powerful position, I would try to do something about it.

When I talk about a powerful position, I am not talking about power in the sense of money. I am talking about the power to motivate, influence and expose them to more than the status quo.

My hope is putting the young men's lives first. Many of them have already been disappointed by at least one man and in contrast we (the people affiliated with this organization) hope to be reliable examples in their lives. We started with five young men and at the time of this publication, we have ended up with over 160. We are building kings!

I would describe mentoring as planting a seed in the ground, watering it, and watching it grow. We plant so many seeds and water those flowers every day. Some may not grow as fast as others but when they blossom you can sit back, like a proud dad, and say, *"Wow! look at this!"*

I have heard everything from young men getting full ride scholarships to one graduating from the Air Force Academy. After growing up some, either they, or their mothers, have said to me,

"Without you, this wouldn't be possible." Mentoring helps the young men develop a strong foundation. To return to the farming analogy, if you have a strong foundation, then you will be able to outlast life's storms.

I tell anyone that wants to start mentoring that you can't be primarily motivated by money. I remember traveling, serving, and speaking for two years without getting a dime. God has a way of providing when needed. I remember being at a point of discouragement with the finances and out of the blue I got a call from a university located in Georgia. They wanted to professionally partner which showed that they recognize my value to their young people.

The transferable concept is that if you have a passion for something don't just talk about it. Make purposeful steps towards creating a solution to address the problem. You don't have to start an organization like I did but do something worthwhile. Start by researching the people or organizations in your area that are helping in your targeted area.

Once you have identified the entities that you want to partner with, reach out to them; send an email, call or text. Share that you have a similar passion and try to be of service. If no similar entity exists near you, consider talking to wise mentors or reading what it would take to launch an organization in your community.

In summary, the TUCK project has been featured on television stations and by many prominent individuals. However, that is not what is most important. What's most important is the growth in the lives of the young men.

I hope that the organization impacts young men to one day start their own nonprofits, go to college, travel, and be the type of men that could improve the lives of their own families.

I also believe that mentorship should start in one's own house. As my dad was my most influential mentor. I am now able to take all the great life lessons that I have shared in this book and give them to the protege that is in my own house, my son.

Chapter 11:
Fatherhood: A New Chapter

As I close out this book, I want to turn my attention to my last chapter towards fatherhood. I am now a father of a son, and my goal is passing the torch to him.

Like my own father, I want to show him that anything is possible. I am his clock, and I must set the example for him. He has given me a reason to set an example to go hard as a professional and a man in general.

He has fired me up and given me a greater reason to leave a legacy. I am the first in my immediate family to go to college and first to start my nonprofit. I want him to see a vision for himself in me. I want him to far exceed or surpass any goal or accomplishment that I have met.

This book is dedicated to him. I hope that he will one day read it and know from whence he came. He will be able to build upon my foundation. He can avoid my mistakes, understand how to build new relationships, and not be limited by other people's low expectations.

Finally, I want you, the reader, to realize how valuable you are. Perspective is key. Don't let others devalue you. You are greater than your worst moments. You are not inferior, you can measure up to a high standard, and you are enough.

About the Author

Terrance Tucker leads the T.U.C.K. Project, mentoring over 170 young men across Columbia, SC, and Augusta, GA since 2016. Alongside leading monthly outreach initiatives aiding the homeless, Terrance is a sought-after speaker at over 200 schools, federal prisons, and juvenile detention centers. His impactful talks inspire and motivate audiences.

A proud graduate of C.A. Johnson High School and South Carolina State University, Terrance intertwines education and empathy in his community efforts. He's been honored with awards like the 2018 South Carolina Black Pages Top 20 under 40 professional, the 2020 Southeastern Association of

Educational Opportunity Program Personnel Conference "TRIO Achiever Award," 2020 Inaugural 40 under 40 Class at South Carolina State University.

Terrance continues to shine as a leader, reflected in his selection to the Leadership Columbia Class of 2023 for his outstanding leadership in the Midlands area. As a dedicated member of Omega Psi Phi Fraternity, Incorporated, he infuses brotherhood values into his impactful work.

Contact the Author

E-mail: Tltuck05@yahoo.com

LinkedIn - Terrance Tucker (Tuck Project, LLC)

M.A.

Facebook - Terrance Tuck Tucker

Instagram- Tuckprojectsc

X - Terrance_tuck

www.Tuckproject.org